God Bless Americana

A retro vacation slide show tour of the USA by Charles Phoenix

Graphic Arts Center Publishing®

Published by Graphic Arts Center Publishing®
An imprint of
Graphic Arts Center Publishing Company
P.O. Box 10306
Portland, OR 97296-0306
503. 226. 2402
www.gacpc.com

Library of Congress Cataloging-in-Publication Data
Phoenix, Charles, 1962–
    God bless Americana / by Charles Phoenix.
      p. cm.
    ISBN 1-55868-644-4
    1. United States—Description and travel. 2. United States—Social life and customs—1945-1970—Pictorial works. 3. United States—History, Local—Pictorial works. 4. Vacations—United States—History—20th century—Pictorial works. 5. Family recreation—United States—History—20th century—pictorial works. 6. Slides (Photography)—United States. I. Title

E169.02 .P48 2002
973.9—dc21   2002022555

President: Charles M. Hopkins
Associate Publisher: Douglas A. Pfeiffer
Editorial Staff: Timothy W. Frew, Tricia Brown, Jean Andrews, Kathy Matthews,
    Jean Bond-Slaughter
Production Staff: Dick Owsiany, Heather Doornink
Design: Kaie Wellman/Cabazon Design
Cartography: Maps.com

Printed and bound in Hong Kong

INTRODUCTION

God Bless Americana is a retro vacation slide show tour of the USA. Travel through time by plane, train, ocean liner, and automobile and see the sights, scenes, and situations that inspired a generation of camera-totin' tourists to snap and click their way across town and country. Visit kitschy tourist traps, classic roadside attractions, big cities, America's heartland, national parks, tropical shores, world's fairs, mom-and-pop motels, and "long lost relatives" along the way.

Los Angeles,
California, 1961

The pictures in the book were not meant to be seen by you and me.

This retro vacation journey takes you around the United States starting "at home" in Los Angeles, across the Southwestern and Southern states, up the East Coast to New England, and back across the Midwestern and Northern states. From there the tour continues up to Alaska, back down through Washington, Oregon, and Northern California, and then across the Pacific Ocean to Hawaii, eventually ending "back home" in Los Angeles.

The pictures in this book were never meant to be seen by you or by me, and certainly were never intended to be published. They were printed from vintage 35mm slides taken by many different tourists on vacations and road trips in the United States between 1940 and 1969. Most of these personal slides were probably shown in the family room once or twice then put away, destined never to see the light of a projector's bulb again . . . until I found them.

Amateur slide photography and the classic American vacation both came of age at about the same time. In 1935, Kodak introduced Kodachrome color slide film developed from 35mm motion picture film. But it wasn't until after World War II, as the country's economy prospered and the masses had extra money to spend, that Kodak began marketing its Kodachrome film to amateur photographers. At the same time, the

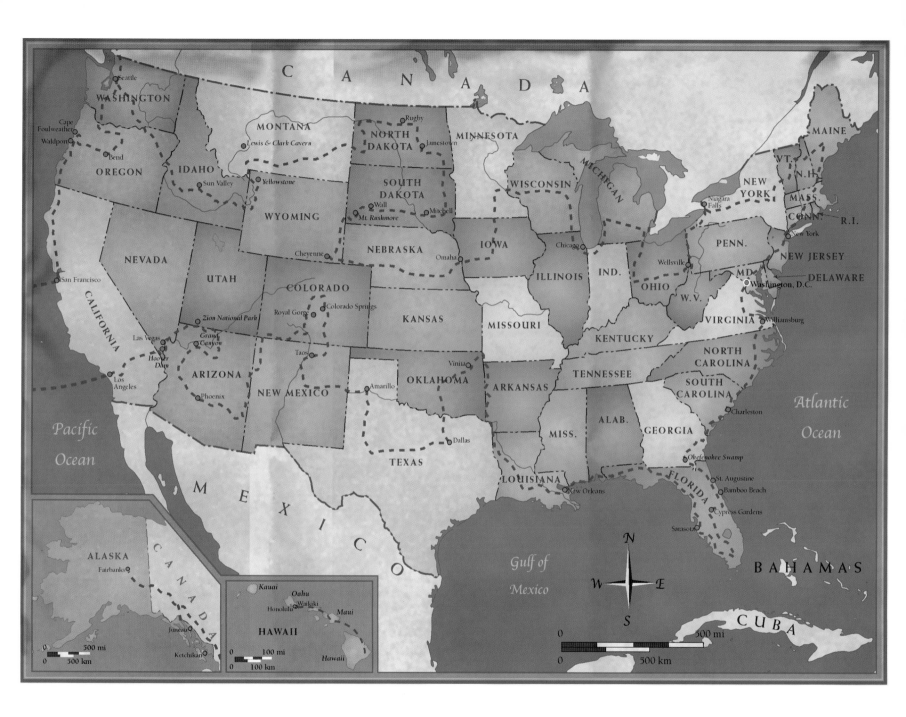

CANADA

WASHINGTON
Seattle

Cape
Foulweather
Waldport
Bend
OREGON
IDAHO
Sun Valley

MONTANA
Lewis & Clark Cavern
Yellowstone

Rugby
NORTH
DAKOTA
Jamestown
MINNESOTA

WYOMING
SOUTH
DAKOTA
Wall
Mt. Rushmore
Mitchell

WISCONSIN
MICHIGAN

MAINE

VT.
N.H.
NEW
YORK
MASS.

NEVADA
UTAH
COLORADO
Cheyenne
NEBRASKA
Omaha
IOWA
Chicago
ILLINOIS
IND.

San Francisco
CALIFORNIA

Zion National Park
Royal Gorge
Colorado Springs

KANSAS
MISSOURI

Niagara
Falls
CONN.
R.I.
New York
PENN.
NEW JERSEY
Wellsville
MD.
DELAWARE
OHIO
Washington, D.C.
W.V.
VIRGINIA
Williamsburg
KENTUCKY

Las Vegas
Hoover
Dam
Grand
Canyon
Taos

Los
Angeles
ARIZONA
Phoenix
NEW MEXICO

Vinita
Amarillo
OKLAHOMA
Dallas
TEXAS

TENNESSEE
ARKANSAS

NORTH
CAROLINA

SOUTH
CAROLINA
Charleston

ALAB.
GEORGIA

Pacific

Ocean

MISS.

Atlantic
Ocean

Okefenokee Swamp

LOUISIANA
FLORIDA
St. Augustine
Bamboo Beach
New Orleans
Cypress Gardens

MEXICO

Sarasota

Gulf of
Mexico

N
W
E
S

BAHAMAS

ALASKA
Fairbanks
CANADA

Kauai
Oahu
Waikiki
Honolulu
Maui
Hawaii

CUBA

Juneau
HAWAII
Ketchikan

0   500 mi
0   500 km

0   100 mi
0   100 km

0   500 mi
0   500 km

The classic American dream vacation had become more than a privilege; it had become a right.

nation greatly expanded its network of highways and byways, and Americans took to the road like never before.

The classic American dream vacation had become more than a privilege, it had become a right. This new mobile society traveled in an age before corporate America ruled the roadside. There were countless home-spun mom-and-pop motels, unique tourist attractions, and other roadside establishments to accommodate and amuse the travelers along the way to wherever they were going. Thankfully, many tourists took their cameras and recorded their trips for posterity.

When I ask for old slides at thrift shops, estate sales, and flea markets, I'm always amazed because the response is always the same.

"What do you do with them?" they ask with puzzled looks on their faces.

"I collect them," I say.

"You collect other people's slides?"

"Yes, I'm an historian, and they are a great way for me to learn about history."

With that said most people still have a hard time understanding why on earth anyone would be interested in looking at old slides taken by perfect strangers.

I first stepped into a thrift shop when I was fourteen years old to look for a cowboy shirt after being cast in the chorus of a community theater production of *Oklahoma!* The possibility of finding unique vintage treasures immediately fascinated me, and I quickly developed a thrift store shopping habit.

After nearly two decades of finding great old clothes, art, home furnishings, and other vintage riches, I stumbled upon an old blue shoe box marked "Trip Across the United States, 1957." The box was full of old 35mm Kodachrome slides. Each one was hand captioned: Cypress Gardens, Florida; The Pigeon Hole Parking Garage, Dallas; Voodoo Vendor, New Orleans; etc.

I held a few up to the light, and I knew instantly I had hit the jackpot and that this stash of old slides was a one-of-a-kind treasure with my name on it. Before someone could say, "hey, those are mine," or "those aren't for sale," I made a mad dash for the cash register and bought them.

The next day I found an old projector. And that evening I projected the slides on my living room wall over and over until the bulb burned out. I was mesmerized. Each slide was like looking through a magic window into the past. I studied every detail in every picture: the cars, the clothes, the places, and most of all the people. I felt I knew these people. They

Most of these personal slides were probably shown in the family room once or twice and then put away . . .

7

The images inspired my imagination, and I learned from them.

reminded me of my own family. I felt so privileged to be able to go along with them on the trip that they had taken more than forty years before. I was looking at real history, the genuine article, something that Hollywood cannot reproduce.

This experience was very enriching. The images inspired my imagination and I learned from them. I couldn't wait to go out and search for more. So in my best seek-and-ye-shall-find mode I began frequenting flea markets, yard sales, estate sales, and thrift shops looking for more "orphan" slides. Much to my surprise, just about every time I went out to hunt, I would find another collection.

Most of the vintage slides I find were taken in the 1950s and '60s, and occasionally there will be some as early as the '40s and some as late as the '70s. Thankfully, most amateur photographers shot their slides with Kodachrome film, which after all of these years, hasn't faded a bit. Those who perhaps didn't want to step up to the more expensive Kodachrome film used cheaper film stock, and over the years the colors of those slides have faded.

Naturally some slide collections are more interesting than others, but I'm still satisfied if a collection yields just one amazing image. Looking through a collection of personal slides, I become very familiar with the people in them and their lifestyle: where they lived, what they drove, where they traveled, and what their interests were. The stories about the people in this book are all true. When I say "she is a mother of twins" or "he lived to be a hundred years old," she really was and he really did. Not every slide is hand captioned by the photographer, so if the name of the person wasn't written on the slide I make one up, like "Mrs. Bobbysocks" or "Mrs. Polehugger."

In the span of a few months, my house became cluttered with boxes full of old slides. With each newfound collection, I would pick out my favorites and proudly share them by having slide shows for friends in my living room. One friend suggested that I have a slide show at a local map and travel store. When I spoke to the owner of the store, he said, "No one would be interested in looking at someone else's old vacation slides." I couldn't believe it. I asked him to look at a few of the vintage slides and then maybe he would change his mind. When he saw them, his eyes lit up just as I knew they would. We agreed on a date for a show.

Next came the task of putting the show together. I went through each slide in every collection picking out my favorites and wondering how I would weave them together to create a story. Mixing and matching my favorite slides together and attempting to create a realistic documentary-type look

I felt I knew these people. They reminded me of my own family . . .

The stories about the people in this book are all true . . .

at midcentury vacation slide photography, I decided to begin the show just as a vacation would begin, by backing out of the driveway at home, then ending the show by arriving back home. I racked my brain trying to come up with a fitting name for the show. I knew that it had to be something patriotic. I thought, *America . . . America the Beautiful . . . God Bless America . . . God Bless Americana . . . That's it!* When I made the presentation, the audience laughed and giggled through the whole thing. And I thought I was being so serious. A couple of weeks later a story about the show appeared in the *Los Angeles Times Sunday Magazine.* And the next time I did the show almost two hundred people showed up. From there I began performing *God Bless Americana* at museums and theaters around Los Angeles.

Now it's your turn to go on this once-in-a-lifetime dream vacation. I invite you to sit back, relax, and enjoy this "trip" back in time as seen through the lens of the tourist.

Los Angeles, California, 1963

The vacation begins, backing out of the driveway.
These people can't wait to start taking pictures!

Las Vegas, Nevada, 1957

Our first stop, the brightest city block west of the Mississippi, Fremont Street in downtown Las Vegas. While the world's largest mechanical sign, "Vegas Vic," waves to us, the Carnival Room at the Fremont, downtown's newest and most modern hotel, welcomes deer hunters.

Las Vegas, Nevada, 1957

Inside, in the middle of the Horseshoe Casino
floor, $1,000,000 is on display: one hundred
$10,000 bills. The lady on the left is trembling; all
that money makes her very nervous. The lady on
the right wearing the flying saucer hat is running
away; she can't stand the sight of a million dollars!

Las Vegas, Nevada, 1957

It's not easy to find a room in Vegas during the Christmas season. For those not lucky enough to get a room in the new Hotel Fremont, the Apache Hotel above the Horseshoe Casino is the second-nicest place to stay downtown. But for those who really prefer something a little more uptown and up-to-date . . .

Las Vegas, Nevada, 1964

... How about the Orbit Inn Motel! In the parking lot in front of that out-of-this-world sign, there are two 1960 Plymouths parked side by side. The low-line Plymouth has one chrome rocket ornament on its fin; the deluxe model has three. Plymouth advertisements claimed the enormous fins were vertical stabilizers.

Las Vegas, Nevada, 1955

This very glamorous couple is visiting Las Vegas from Hollywood.
He's a soundman for the movies, and she's a purse designer.
They're always impeccably dressed. Even by the pool she's
fully accessorized. She won't go swimming, but he will.

Las Vegas, Nevada, 1951

Speaking of well dressed, this is Dolly wearing a smart red-and-white-striped bathing suit. She breeds Dalmatians. She is having the open-face fried shrimp sandwich platter served with onion rings, lettuce, ketchup, and milk, poolside at the Thunderbird on the Las Vegas Strip.

Las Vegas, Nevada, 1961

Poolside at the Sahara, also on the strip, the guy in
the back row is getting too much sun. The guy in
the middle is catching up on the news, and the guy
in the front row, seventh from the right, is having a
nightmare . . . He lost everything the night before.

Las Vegas, Nevada, 1969

This is the feeling you get after drinking too many free screwdrivers and eating too many free shrimp cocktails at the Circus Circus!

Hoover Dam, Nevada, 1964

My girdle is killing me! These are the Shapely Sisters. One goes positive, and one goes negative.

Hoover Dam, Nevada, 1940

I have no idea who this character is. He's wearing a long, fringed Western jacket, matching fringed pants tucked into high lace-up boots, scarf, hand-painted pouch, twin holsters packed with pistols, finished with a thin red walking stick and topped off by a fez. Is he on his way to a Shriner's Western theme party? Or is he a Shriner obsessed with Daniel Boone?

Arizona, 1954

This is "Mr. and Mrs. Bobbysocks"
on their way to the Grand Canyon. Either
they're in a big hurry to get there, or . . .

Arizona, 1954

. . . "Mrs. Bobbysocks" is just learning
how to drive.

Arizona, 1954

The couple on the left is two feet inside the Grand Canyon, the people in the middle are two feet from the edge, and "Mrs. Bobbysocks" is holding on for dear life. She's as petrified as the wood she's sitting on!

Phoenix, Arizona, 1952

It's Easter Sunday, and this lovely lady and her best friend Mary-Charlotte are staying at a charming little motel. They're going to spend the holiday having a few cocktails out on the lawn.

Phoenix, Arizona, 1952

Mary-Charlotte has turned the bathroom into a make-shift bar. Kahlua and tequila with a squeeze, anyone?

Phoenix, Arizona, 1952

Later that afternoon, Mary-Charlotte is just fine—
she's still sitting up—but her friend is sucking
foam out of the lawn furniture!

Taos, New Mexico, 1957

"Real Pueblo Indians" pose proudly
between performing "Native tribal dances"
for tourists—but in a parking lot?

New Mexico-Utah border, 1952

This is Carl, a bachelor aerospace engineer traveling in his brand new metallic green '52 Chevrolet Bel Air. Later, if he needs a rest stop, he should look for . . .

Zion National Park, Utah, 1957

. . . the peepee teepees!

Utah, 1946

This is Dolly, the Dalmatian breeder, wearing thick black wool with genuine leopard-fur collar, hat, and muff—the perfect ensemble for viewing the world's largest open pit copper mine.

**Royal Gorge,
Colorado, 1950**

Hold on for dear life!
We're onboard "the world's
steepest incline railway"
on the very steep way
down to the bottom of
the Royal Gorge.

Royal Gorge, Colorado, 1950

Once you get down to the bottom there's absolutely nothing to do but wait to get back up to the top.

Colorado Springs, Colorado, 1964

A heavenly light shines on United States Air Force Academy Cadet Chapel. Appropriately, it looks like seventeen jet fighters stacked side by side. It was dedicated in 1963 to the future officers of the United States Air Force.

Vinita, Oklahoma, 1962

Gracefully spanning the Will Rogers Turnpike, this is the world's fastest drive-through, the Glass House Restaurant. It was built in 1957, and, surprisingly, it's still standing today as the world's largest McDonald's, with the world's largest golden arches.

Tulsa, Oklahoma, 1953

Here we are at Tulsa's International Petroleum Exhibition, which began in 1923. Making his debut here thirty years later, the famous "Golden Driller" towers over the festivities. He looks like a giant Academy Award wearing a hard hat and saying, "How sweet it is."

Tulsa, Oklahoma, 1959

In 1959, a hundred years after America's first commercial oilwell was drilled in Pennsylvania, the look was out-of-this-world as the International Petroleum Exhibition celebrated "100 years of petroleum progress." Tulsa was known for oil even before Oklahoma became a state. In 1905, drillers hit a gusher just southeast of town. Soon the area was flooded with oilmen and companies looking to get rich quick. Many did. And by the 1920s Tulsa was the "oil capital of the world."

Tulsa, Oklahoma, 1959

Dinner with the relatives—roast turkey and ambrosia. Ambrosia is that American culinary classic blend of fruit cocktail, marshmallows, coconut, and Cool Whip. What happened to the stuffing and mashed potatoes and gravy? "Miss Pearl-headband" doesn't care; she's going to smoke her dinner!

Texas, 1964

This is "Mrs. Polehugger" gettin' her kicks on Route 66.
She holds on to signposts everywhere she goes.

Amarillo, Texas, 1949

At the Sunset Motel on Route 66, accommodations include "well kept rooms with modern furnishings, wall-to-wall carpeting, cross ventilation, private baths, baby beds, and a shaded playground." The rooms have no phones, no television, and no air conditioning. There is no swimming pool, no cable, and "No Vacancy. Sorry"!

Dallas, Texas, 1957

Behind the Statler Hilton Hotel, the new Pigeon Hole Parking Garage is completely ultra-modern and up-to-date. It's "Automatic . . . lock your car . . . take your keys . . . fast . . . safe . . . no ramps," yes . . . and no guardrails either.

New Orleans, Louisiana, 1959

**A mother of twins visits the Voodoo
Vendor in the famous French Quarter
for all of her voodoo needs.**

New Orleans, Louisiana, 1959

Stepping off the curb to admire a painting can be very dangerous. Perhaps "Mrs. Flatbottom" doesn't hear the roar of that big Chevrolet V-8. If she steps back any farther, she's going to be "Mrs. Flatterbottom"!

Georgia, 1955

Ruth, Rose, and Delores are frolicking in their
Okefenokee swamp-side motel room. Their
friend Flo doesn't want to play with them . . .

Georgia, 1955

. . . She wants to play outside,
in "America's most primitive
swamp." She's a real nature
freak. She is . . .

Georgia, 1955

. . . the Swamp Thing!

Florida, 1955

This is the classic "butt-out" shot taken at one of Florida's six official welcome stations. Inside, tourists rest and relax while attractive young hostesses serve free chilled orange juice and answer any questions visitors may have about the Sunshine State.

Florida, 1957

While homemade cheese pizza is prepared for the guests poolside at the Bamboo Beach Motel, the owner's son dons a chef's hat and serenades everyone with his fancy new accordion.

St. Augustine, Florida, 1957

"The best way to see St. Augustine," the oldest city in the United States, is from a striped-canvas-canopy-shaded-yellow-sightseeing tram. Adults $1.50, Children 75 cents.

Winter Haven, Florida, 1957

After performing together in the "world famous"
water ski shows at Cypress Gardens, the
aquamaids and aquamen pose proudly for pictures.

Florida, 1956

At Weeki Wachee, Florida's underwater Grand Canyon, beautiful young ladies train for three months to earn the right to be called Weeki Wachee Mermaids. When they graduate from mermaid school, they receive their diplomas underwater.

Sarasota, Florida, 1956

This is the winter home of "The Greatest Show on Earth," the Ringling Bros. Barnum & Bailey Circus. The main attraction? The world's largest herd of baby elephants.

Florida, 1955

**Hey seagull, stay away from that lady—
She's a taxidermist!**

Florida, 1955

I hope there's not going to be a catfight over who gets to take that beautiful seagull centerpiece home.

Miami, Florida, 1957

"Welcome to Parrot Jungle,
where thousands of tropical
birds fly free, yet eat from your
hand and pose on your arms"
. . . and shoulders . . . and head.

South Carolina, 1957

This basket weaver is a master of her craft.
She is selling her wares roadside just
outside of Charleston, South Carolina.

North Carolina, 1952

When Carl, the bachelor engineer, gets tired of driving, no problem, he just pulls over on the side of the road, pitches his pup tent, and waits for someone with a foot fetish to pass by.

Williamsburg, Virginia, 1964

Remember "Mrs. Polehugger"? This is "Mr. Polehugger," experiencing the proudest moment of his life!

Washington, D.C., 1963

A man stands proud taking a picture of the Iwo Jima Memorial. More United States Marines earned the Medal of Honor on Iwo Jima than in any other battle in U.S. history.

Washington, D.C., 1968

This is Violet on the steps of the Jefferson Memorial. She is traveling up the East Coast in her Volkswagen Bug. The purple suit must make her feel like a million bucks, because she wears it everywhere she goes. The fashionable look is complete with matching shoes, purse, and gloves.

Washington, D.C., 1958

"In This Temple As In The Hearts Of The People For Whom He Saved The Union The Memory Of Abraham Lincoln Is Enshrined Forever." I wonder what the four ladies in the matching white beanie caps think of that?

New York, New York, 1951

From high atop the Statue of Liberty, America's most famous combination monument and observation tower, this is a picture-perfect view of the city. In 1951, the Giants won the pennant, *The King and I* opened on Broadway, and RCA made the first color television broadcast from the Empire State Building.

New York, New York, 1951

The heart of New York City, Times Square, the most electrified crossroads in the world. There's magic in the air, the traffic is streaming by, and Uncle Sam Wants You!

New York World's Fair, 1964

Standing fourteen stories tall and made entirely out of stainless steel, this is the Unisphere, the symbol of the 1964 World's Fair. Hey, who forgot to put up the flags?

New York World's Fair, 1964

While riding in the sky buckets and taking in the bird's-eye view of the fair, one has time to ponder the theme of the fair: "Man in a shrinking globe in an expanding universe." Whatever that means.

New York World's Fair, 1964

"Mrs. Polehugger" says "cheese."
She just can't resist.

New York, New York, 1968

Violet wants to look her best while visiting Chinatown, so she is wearing her favorite purple suit . . . again! She's been wearing it since Washington, D.C. What happened to her gloves? Did she forget them in the restaurant? Maybe she took them off because the chopsticks kept slipping out of her hands.

New Hampshire, 1957

**In New England, the colors are
beginning to change . . .**

New Hampshire, 1968

. . . but Violet's not. By now that suit is wearing her!
Has she lost her shoes now too?

Bellows Falls, Vermont, 1953

This is the distinguished Earl H. Christian,
relaxing on his five-hundred-acre farm.
He is sporting a stylish striped robe and
matching cap. He drives the Jeep.

Bellows Falls, Vermont, 1953

This is the lovely Mrs. Earl H. Christian. She
drives the big black Buick Roadmaster and carries
a shotgun. She wears the pants in the family ...

**Bellows Falls,
Vermont, 1953**

. . . like I said, she wears the
pants in the family!

Maine, 1960

Looks like there is a little more available at the
Farmer's Daughter Gift Barn than New England crafts,
gloves, moccasins, furniture, and maple syrup!

Niagara Falls, New York, 1957

"Seeing Niagara Falls from the deck of
the *Maid of the Mist* is the most satisfactory and
complete way of viewing the famous cataracts. The
$1.10 fare includes tax and waterproof clothing."

Niagara Falls, New York, 1952

This is Margie and Dick on their honeymoon at Niagara Falls, the "honeymoon capital of the world."

Wellsville, Ohio, 1957

**All is well in the picture-perfect,
riverside town of Wellsville . . .**

Wellsville, Ohio, 1957

. . . Junior's wearing his cuffed Levi's and T-shirt
with rolled sleeves, Missy's wearing her pedal
pusher-toreador-capri-clamdigger pants, mama's
wearing her three-quarter car coat, and daddy,
well, he's wearing his pants halfway up to his chin!

Chicago, Illinois, 1957

The view of the skyline is magnificent from Grant Park. The canna lilies are in full bloom, the grass is green, and the trees are full. When the Prudential Building was completed in 1955, the ultramodern forty-one-story skyscraper was the pride of the Chicago skyline and the tallest building in town.

Muskegon, Michigan, 1953

This classic hostess-with-the-mostess
serves white cake, sliced ham, rye bread,
cling peaches on a bed of lettuce . . . and a
big beautiful bowl of delicious ambrosia.

Wisconsin, 1957

At the Gilbert E. Lenz Farm, the little aluminum cow on the mailbox is more than decoration. It signifies the fact that they have cattle. The toilet float on top is also more than decoration; it's a status symbol. It's a sign to everyone who passes by: they have indoor plumbing!

Wisconsin, 1968

On the farm they drink a lot of milk and eat a lot of corn. And on that plate, a little ham, a little yam to go with the ham, and a delicious helping of ... ambrosia. I looked up ambrosia in the dictionary, and I couldn't believe what it said: "mythological food of the gods."

Omaha, Nebraska,
1948

At Boys Town, you know
what Father Flanagan says,
"There is no such thing
as a bad boy."

Nebraska, 1956

These fine young men are on an outing
on the Missouri River near Boys Town.
Don't ask, don't tell!

South Dakota, 1962

**"Welcome to South Dakota.
The Land of Infinite Variety"?**

South Dakota, 1962

Here it is in all of its breathtaking reality—distinguishable from over sixty miles away, the shrine of democracy— Mt. Rushmore. Begun in 1927, it took fourteen years to sculpt these monumental images of George Washington, Thomas Jefferson, Theodore Roosevelt, and Abraham Lincoln.

Wall, South Dakota, 1962

"On a hot summer day a cold glass of water can be the summit of man's desire. But who ever heard of making a fortune out of it?" Well, Ted and Dorothy Hustead did. In 1936, Dorothy came up with the idea to lure passing motorists into their drugstore by posting signs along the highway advertising free ice water. Soon the legendary "Free Ice Water, Wall Drug" signs were posted in almost every state in the nation and in foreign countries around the world.

Mitchell, South Dakota, 1965

Covered completely in dried-out corncobs, grains, and grasses,
this is the Mitchell Corn Palace, "America's greatest agricultural
monument." It was built in 1921 to show off South Dakota's fertile
soil. It looks like a cross between the Kremlin and the Taj Majal.

Rugby, North Dakota, 1963

This glorified spotlit pile of rocks is the geographical center of North America . . . and a dangerous obstacle in the middle of a parking lot.

Jamestown, North Dakota, 1962

After a long day on the range and being dwarfed by the world's largest buffalo, these men are looking forward to stretching out in their cabin . . .

North Dakota, 1962

**. . . Their '61 Chevrolet Impala is bigger than the
cabin. They should've stayed in the car.**

Wyoming, 1967

This is Helen, a switchboard operator for the phone company. She is a trinket junkie and a souvenir shopaholic about to go on a shopping spree.

Wyoming, 1952

This fine gentleman loved
to fish and hunt and pose
with his kill or catch of
the day. He lived to be
one hundred years old.

Yellowstone, Wyoming, 1954

Old Faithful is the biggest star of Yellowstone. It was named in 1870 for its unfailing regularity. The legendary eruption never fails to draw a crowd. This crowd dressed up for the occasion.

Yellowstone, Wyoming, 1957

At Yellowstone, America's oldest and grandest national park, the sight of a mama bear and her baby cub cause the driver of a bullet-nosed '51 Studebaker to pull over on the wrong side of the road. The lady in the Ford doesn't look too happy about that.

Yellowstone, Wyoming, 1954

A man taunting a bear.
The folks back home will never believe this.

Montana, 1956

A plaid jacket with bias cut patch pockets over a floral print skirt—straight from the runways of Paris to the depths of Montana's Lewis and Clark Cavern.

Sun Valley, Idaho, 1950

"Give me your tired, your
poor, your huddled masses
yearning to breathe free" . . .
quick, I'm melting!

Seattle World's Fair, Washington, 1962

The Space Needle, the icon of the 1962 World's Fair, was designed to resemble a flying saucer. The original design concept was sketched on a cocktail napkin in a bar.

Seattle World's Fair, Washington, 1962

This is the United States Science Pavilion. It was "the $10,000,000 prediction of the world of tomorrow. . . . The most extensive and startling scientific achievement ever assembled."

Fairbanks, Alaska, 1958

After the "Welcome to Statehood" parade, everyone
will drink Budweiser and Hamm's beer. In 1867,
the United States purchased Alaska from Russia
for $7,200,000. That's about two cents an acre.

Juneau, Alaska, 1962

In Alaska, tourists love to pose with giant totem poles. Tourists that really love totem poles . . .

Alaska, 1948

. . . become totem poles.

Ketchikan, Alaska, 1950

This is a rush-hour traffic jam in downtown
Ketchikan, "the salmon capital of the world."

Alaska, 1955

The dress code for traveling on the Alaska Railroad between Fairbanks and Anchorage: suits and ties for the men, and coats, hats, and high heels for the ladies.

Washington, 1960

Back in Washington at the Richfield Gas Station it's
time to gas up the '55 Buick. Fill 'er up with ethyl.
I hope he has the five dollars to cover that!

Bend, Oregon, 1955

Here at Peterson's Rock Garden, a spectacular folk art
environment near Bend, the tourist and the tourist
attraction are a perfect match. They're color coordinated.

Waldport, Oregon, 1961

This is a proper picnic dinner in Oregon: Dungeness crab, potato salad, oyster crackers, a Washington apple, pickled peppers, chili sauce. And to wash it all down . . . a couple quarts of Olympia beer. What? No ambrosia?

Oregon, 1961

"You'll remember the lookout on Cape Foulweather, where Oregon history began. . . . See White Sea Lions through the telescope." Those people aren't looking at White Sea Lions down there on the beach . . .

Oregon, 1959

. . . they're looking at this bathing beauty. She made her bathing suit. In fact she does real well with women's swimwear, but she doesn't do too well with men's swimwear . . .

Oregon, 1959

. . . Underwear and a scrap
of striped fabric safety-
pinned together. Perhaps he
should've gone for a fitting.

Oregon, 1962

In 1965, the First Lady, Lady Bird Johnson,
championed the national Highway Beautification Act
to eliminate what she called distasteful roadside
signs. Certainly she wasn't thinking of signs like this.

Northern California, 1948

At the Trees of Mystery along the Redwood Highway, "See unreal realities. See the trees that you read about in *Ripley's Believe it or Not* and saw in *Universal Newsreels*. Paul Bunyan directs you through the hollow entrance log on a tour of mysteriously formed trees to be seen nowhere else in the world."

Northern California, 1948

Along the Redwood Highway, Dolly, the
Dalmatian breeder, parks her '48 Plymouth and
poses under the Chandelier Tree, the world's
oldest drive-through—2,500 years old.

San Francisco, California, 1949

**This is Joe, posing in the classic
"walk-way-over-there-and-I'll-take-your-picture"
shot at the famous and historic Cliff House
overlooking the Seal Rocks.**

San Francisco, California, 1958

Behind the Cliff House, a very heavy sky tram stresses a glorified clothesline strung over the Seal Rocks. The ladder below is there for the search and rescue team.

San Francisco, California, 1956

**All Aboard! From the deck of the grand ocean liner S.S. *Lurline*
docked in San Francisco, bound for Honolulu, Hawaii. This
is the "I'm-going-to-Hawaii-and-you're-not" shot. Bon Voyage!**

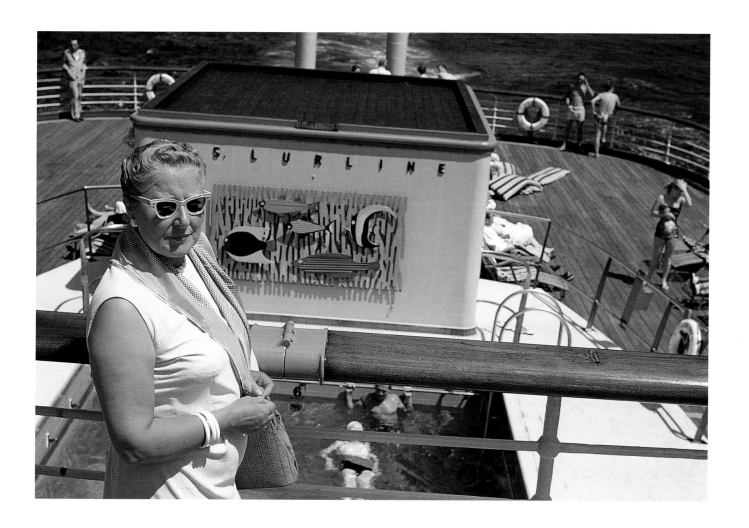

On the Pacific Ocean, 1956

This is "Smiley," traveling in luxurious first-class comfort aboard the S.S. *Lurline* on her way to a Shriner's convention at Waikiki with her husband. She is a very well-to-do world traveler. She never smiles.

Hawaii, 1956

Donning their Hawaiian duds, high atop
Waikiki's Hawaiian Village rooftop,
Dot and Dan say, "Aloha."

Hawaii, 1956

For most tourists, stopping at a roadside pineapple stand is a
special treat. Looks like this woman has never tried the exotic
fruit before. "Smiley" is second from the left; she is not smiling.

Hawaii, 1966

My, what good taste you have. On the beach at Maui, these two women showed up wearing matching yellow swimsuits. Which one went to charm school?

Hawaii, 1949

This young tourist poses with his Royal Hawaiian surfboard ready to hit the waves at Waikiki. He has never surfed in his life. The surfboard is solid redwood and weighs a ton.

Hawaii, 1963

The Luau look for 1963: a tight red-and-white Hawaiian dress with ruffled sleeve and flounce, matching flowered lei and hibiscus head ornament, jet black cat-eye glasses, and, in place of an evening bag . . . a live turtle.

Hawaii, 1960

While waiting for the roast
suckling pig to be served, the
friendly aloha spirit overcomes
this man and fills him with lust.
He squeezes his wife's arm
and tries to kiss a pretty young
lady. The young lady cringes,
yet smiles politely, as she rolls
her right eye.

Hawaii, 1963

"Ask not what your country can do for you, but what you can do for your country." President Kennedy visited Hawaii on July 9, 1963.

Hawaii, 1956

Just before leaving Hawaii, "Smiley" strikes a pose beneath the sharp propeller blades. Hey, "Smiley," back up just a little bit more.

Between Hawaii and California, 1962

High in the sky as we fly back home to Los Angeles, I dedicate this book to all of the unsuspecting camera-totin' tourists that captured history while snapping and clicking their way across our great country. To them and to you I say, "God Bless Americana."

Los Angeles, California, 1957

Violet made this.